MW00709981

# A Woman's Guide to Mountain Climbing

*To Ellen,
with pleasure
in long friendship ~*

*June*

*New York City    18 April 2012*

42/30  F. 66.                    Jakob Demmy,                    19488

JANE AUGUSTINE

# A Woman's Guide to Mountain Climbing

◄( poems )►

*Marsh Hawk Press   New York   2008*

COPYRIGHT © 2008 BY JANE AUGUSTINE

All rights reserved.
No part of this book may be reproduced in any form or by any means,
electronic or mechanical, including printing, photocopying, recording,
or by any information storage or retrieval system, without permission
in writing from the publisher.

07 08 09 10 11 12 7 6 5 4 3 2 1 FIRST EDITION

Marsh Hawk Press books are published by Poetry Mailing List, Inc.,
a not-for-profit corporation under section 501 (c) 3 United States
Internal Revenue Code.

*"Lapis Lazuli" drypoint by Jakob Demus,*
*"Wet Mountain Valley" watercolor by Jane Augustine,*
*author photo by Michelle Hood,*
*and book design by Claudia Carlson.*
*The text of this book is set in Fairfield.*

LIBRARY OF CONGRESS CATALOGING-IN-PUBLICATION DATA

Augustine, Jane.
  A woman's guide to mountain climbing : poems / by Jane Augustine.
—1st ed.
    p.  cm.
ISBN-13: 978-0-9792416-5-9 (pbk.)
ISBN-10: 0-9792416-6-9 (pbk.)
  I. Title.
PS3551.U388W66 2008
811'.54–dc22

2007041741

P.O. BOX 206
EAST ROCKAWAY, NEW YORK 11518-0206
www.marshhawkpress.org

# Acknowledgements

The author wishes to thank the New York State Council on the Arts Creative Artists in Public Service program for two Fellowships in Poetry that assisted the completion of this book, and the following editors and publications in which a number of these poems appeared, sometimes under slightly differing titles.

In chapbooks: "Gentians," "Nightsong for Two Voices" and "My Father's Death," appeared in a limited fine-art chapbook designed and printed by Walter Hamady, titled *Lit By the Earth's Dark Blood* (Perishable Press, Mount Horeb, Wisconsin, 1977). "The Passes," "Method," "For Patrick, My Son," "Autumn Meditation" (under the title "For Meg") and "A Bracelet of Turquoise from Aguilar." in issue #2 (Jan. 1985) of *Staple Diet* (Pig Press, Durham, UK), edited by Richard Caddel.

In anthologies: "A Bracelet of Turquoise from Aguilar" and four sections of "Cloud, Rock, Scroll" in *Beneath a Single Moon: Buddhism in Contemporary American Poetry*, eds. Kent Johnson and Craig Paulenich, Boston & London: Shambhala, 1991; "Anti-Cycle for the New Year" in *Long Island Poets*, ed., Robert Long, Sag Harbor, NY: Permanent Press, 1986.

"Cloud, Rock, Scroll" in full originally appeared in *The Iowa Review* 16:3, the H.D. Centennial issue, Fall 1986, edited by Adalaide Morris.

"At Midmonth" was the recipient of a 1975 Poetry in Public Places award and was exhibited at the City University of New York in large placard format. "Rationale" appeared in *MS*.; "At Midmonth" in *Aphra*; "Carrying One's Weight" in *Chrysalis*; "After Yeats" in *Woman Poet: The East*; "Anti-cycle for the New Year" in *The Atlantic Review* (London); "Mayday and All" in *Confrontation*; "My Father's Death" in *Tarasque*; "On Loss," "Cragmont Avenue Childhood" and "The Stars" in *Montemora*; "Rosita Cemetery" in *California Quarterly*; "Waking in Front of a Cracked Mirror" and "By Night" (under the title "Night Life") in *Manhattan Poetry Review*; "Gentians" in *Pequod*; "Western Gothic Romantic Classic," "Mountain Death-Camas," "The Thimble" and "A Winter's Night" in *The Painted Bride Quarterly*; "Limousine" in *The Periodical Lunch* (under the title "Apparitions"); "Continuing" and "Visitation" in *Poetry Northwest*; "Gear" and "Digression on Trailbikers" in *Poetry Now*; "Fireweed" and "Locoweed" in *Snakeroot* (Pratt Institute, Brooklyn). "Autumn Meditation" also appeared under the title "For Meg" in a Poetry Society of America bulletin with favorable commentary by Carolyn Kizer.

Many thanks go as well to the editors of Marsh Hawk Press, especially Burt Kimmelman for specific help with this manuscript, to Claudia Carlson for her special artist's eye in design, and to Michael Heller for enduring kindness and support.

*In memory of my parents*


*Marguerite St. Clair Augustine Radloff*
*(1897–1987)*

*and*

*Waldemar Rolf Herbert Augustine*
*(1899–1975)*

The high peak at night holds back the sun,
The deep vales are never bright by day.
Natural for mountain people to grow straight:
Where paths are steep the mind levels.

> —Meng Chiao (751–841)
> *Wandering on Mount Chung-nan*
> tr. A.C. Graham

# CONTENTS

# ◄ PART I ►

*Journey*

# The Passes: Hardscrabble, Independence

*Pass: a narrow passage, opening,*
*or way through, esp. between mountains; gap; defile*
— Colorado: A Guide to the Highest State

(i)

Beginnings
        can't be seen
                until an ending.

On the road out of town
        bleak prairie blanches to dirt
                split by arroyos—here the Arapahoe

drove back the Ute into Hardscrabble Pass,
        road rising so slowly one doesn't
                notice    then steep narrow

tree-clotted, the sun cut off
        by the overhang of Suicide Spire
                named for a pair of teenaged lovers

—old tales perhaps have lost their power—

from Hardscrabble
        first sight of the mountains:
                snow-summits blur into cloud.

        (ii)

Independence Pass closed in winter,
        but this is late spring—
                snow up higher maybe—

but risk the turnoff.
        Brute tractors
                swarm over mud-mountains    gears

clash   earth's gashed, mauled into
            a dam, power for the Arkansas
                    Fryingpan. A lake's displaced.

        I detour round its draining.

            (iii)

Independence Pass open in summer—
        snow plows have just broken through—

colder than I've ever been, and clear
        Free I say    not to need

            or be familial, generous.

A brink.

No end to wind's buffeting.

            (iv)

Down the Divide by dark:
        waters of the Roaring Fork
                plunge downward with me

run both ways, some back
        to the Diversion Tunnel
                and the Fryingpan, some west

I don't know which:
        by moonlight pass the blackened
                bones of roofless shacks

where a deluded few still come
        gold-hunting—

Independence: a ghost town.

(v)

*in eclipse*

Lost Man Campground:
green firewood burns smoky and goes out.

The waning moon's malformed; darkness bites
into her left side. On rough grass at meadow's edge

I try to sleep. The larches rustle.
An anchorite might wake at 2 a.m. to say

an office, but I've no rule of life. Committed
by default to night and cold, my wakefulness

is mere disease. This road's not on the map
of "the highest state." The moon's a mirror

hung with a sable veil.
Someone is mourned. In darkness

something seems to bend over me,
 a branch perhaps that dips and breathes

(amorphous as remembering,
 which the self-exiled must not)—a warm breath...

shock then   that it grows solid,
a human head, gross body, some other camper

stumbling in wilderness,
some clumsy drunk who'll clutch at anything.

My suffering double begs my bed.
Why not, I think. The sky's a stranger too,

who's snuffed her lamp. I'm free

(vi)

I knew a woman, a Jew and refugee,
        who until the war's end hid
                in a Bavarian cave,

subsisted on roots and berries, then
        married an angry man, but rich. She lived
                better in America.

Here's hermitage—a cabin at road's end,
        once ours, abandoned in midwinter
                so the plumbing's shattered.

The solitary has to hike to the outhouse,
        haul buckets from the pump—
                a clean start over.

Mountain passes    not peaks
        but straits    limiting, hard to get through.
                Hard is what makes it possible.

One enters another country under
        moon and sun, eyes of the world
                that never close. Resources here:

the well goes down a hundred feet, power line's
        connected, stove takes wood.
                Snow falls for three days, covers all.

The mind snowed in    not free
        yet not in a prison camp
                rests in its meditative cave.

Nothing is lost.

I don't know the end of that woman's
        story, heard she'd become depressed
                and left him.

                                Refuge is journey
—so to begin.

# Toward Break of Night, a Dream

*The song was used for curing, and was given to
the poet (Owl Woman, called  Juana Manwell)...*

—Technicians of the Sacred

(i)

Fog. A man on the dock. Creak of hawsers. Spray at the porthole a
mouth twisted against glass
and falling away

      The stateroom door unfastens each time the deck tips too
steeply. I fasten it again and again.

(ii)

Airfield. Stumbling in shiny shocking-pink heels, I run crosscountry
to catch the Alaska jet, taxiing for takeoff

      The pilot opens the cockpit for me, but my leather coat is
missing and no mastercard to charge a new one.

(iii)

The full moon crashes toward me, a stone-shod brewery horse to roll
my skull over in the furrows. Because I lost the saddlebags

      I fall under his hooves. My father's low wall and my mother's
pear trees do nothing to stop him.

(iv)

He stands among oleanders with a revolver. Weeping I pick up my
infant son unconscious and carry him in among jukeboxes and whisky.

      The pay phone dial sticks. The line is dead. I scream and
scream. Men at the bar turn and stare.

(v)

*and wake outside the house while inside shadows still brush the
curtains. Unarmed, must I move only to cold country*

*Owl woman, see for me in the dark what I hold and release. Free me to
live by the body's sources.*

# A Woman's Guide to Mountain Climbing

*nine steps to start with*

## I. GEAR

A woman can carry
on her back
everything needed to survive—

> tent, sweater, sleeping bag
> canteen, flyrod, cheese
> cookpot, poncho, map
> tampons, bowie knife
> and book of stars

can't climb
without these essentials

almost can't climb
with them

## II. RATIONALE

If someone asks
> why you're climbing
> say
> you have the moon
> in mind
> each night
> she meets
> these barrier peaks
> with her eye
> more fully open

> and undersea
> clenched in the shell's night

the pearl persists
in shaping her moon
around

a central irritant

## III. METHOD

Must

      start

            slow    to stay strong

      past the first switch-
back            take abnormally short steps
      boot-toe to heel    no more lift

      than barely clears the ground    hunch
forward to ease the pack-strain
      of lone effort
                  watch

      don't step onto any root or stone
that you can step around
      a stubbed toe dislocates the whole

      backbone    don't stop to rest—
to start again is harder
                    just

      keep moving by
          almost not
              moving    but

don't resist:

      no choice of method
nor to improvise    the path's external, practical
      thus discover, not invent

technique is all:
      less why than how
          you climb

up   out   beyond tree-line
and the last wind-twisted cypress
      past trail's end in scree and talus

to confront the mountain:

nothing

      but rock:
earth's scooped-out skull   its juts
     and fractures sharpened

in the over-bright and nearly non-sustaining air

## IV. DIGRESSION ON TRAILBIKERS

Revving motors outroar the waterfall.
Trailbikers in plastic bubble helmets

leap over the rise. Their goggles
protect them from the dangerous green

of aspen and alpine fir. They're teaching
their sons how to smash through underbrush

and wipe out silence. But now what
unnatural sight confronts them? A woman

carrying her misshapen world on her back.
They flex their nailhead gloves, pretend

to smile, say "You've got a long
walk ahead of you." She says "Longer than

you think: over the peak. Can't get there
except on foot. Takes days." They look

blankly at her madness, voom and leap away.
Of course there's nothing—is there?—

that those engines between their thighs
can't climb to and back from in half an hour

## V. CONTINUING

Too far above trees. Too far above
        the last campsite. Nothing but steepness.
                No firewood, no wind-shelter.

The ridge hides the peak. Must rest
        every ten steps, fall to elbows and knees
                under the minimum needed to survive.

Only the smallest plants live here—
        too little air. My eye tries
                to magnify them, tiny bright blue hopes.

Lungs rasp. Shoulders collect knives.
        Not strong enough to go on.
                But what to do

when it's as hard to climb down
        as up? Shove off the pack a while.
                Lie flat. Try to sleep. The moon

also sleeps at times. Hides out.
        Then begins to climb again, the night
                strapped to her spine. Climbs and keeps

        climbing

## VI  On the Ridge

*12,800 in the Sangré de Cristo mountains*

At sunset your pumping heart
brings you to the ridge:

the point where you can
at least stand up

the mountain that threatened to fall
on you now under foot

the boot's fulcrum no razor's edge
but street-wide

paved with saxifrage whose threads
sunder the granite:

Standing you look west   down
to where night already gathers

in an unknown basin deep
among unnamed peaks

at eye-level still lit
by flaming day   more deserted

strange and lovely than the way
        you came by:

                Deer have carved a trail
                to a glacial pool

                where you follow   make camp
                provisional facing moonrise

                rest up for the next
                riskier   more solitary climb

## VII. VISITATION

*the moon in Sagittarius*

Sleeping, tentflap half-open,
moon on my forehead

a woman shrieks far away
and again—wildcat waking me.

Night breeds
creatures to encircle me.

I came from known dangers
into these:

ground tremor reaches me
before the sound

of hooves on rock
breath in frenzy, snorting

pawing outside
the tent's back corner—

I'm in his path—
too terrified to rise,

face what I fear—
shapeless threat, a beast

ruler of this place
where I'm intruder—

face old fears that grow
of violence, injury

who'll care for me?
how shall I get well?

Helplessness holds me
tight under cover.

When a bear attacks they say
play dead.

I hide until that animal rage
baffled moves off through the willows

and come awake fully then,
slowly regret the chance lost

to stand up living eye to eye
find it after all merely

a white-tailed deer
also terrified

*Here in the courtyard of the moon*
*                    why did I fail to trust her?*

            I push back the tentflap
            climb out:

There she rides
high on the mountain's saddle

helmeted, bow drawn
and quiver full of stars

## VIII. CARRYING ONE'S WEIGHT

### (i)

Impossible
to carry a backpack
equal to one's body weight:

a woman should not carry
more than one-fifth
of what she weighs    a man one-third

I've put aside
the lady's light packframe
and silky nylon bag    choose a heftier

man's size with tough rucksack and shelfbar
sling a walking stick under it
to lift this excessive

33 pounds to my 117

### (ii)

Carrying one's weight:
not dumping shit, tears, chores, claims
on others:

nor foot-dragging—as if you imagined, sir,
your pith helmet guarantees you
a native carrier

### (iii)

A woman often carries more
than her own weight—
the child's too

in the pit of her stomach
and balanced heavily upon
her watchful head: a long safari—

and think of those men who carry none
of their own weight,
who float asleep on the inner springs

of their mothers' curls,
whose bathtubs' crows-feet
are their secretaries' hands and knees

that gray elephant of women's service
bearing up the weight
of the blue-jeweled globe

(iv)

Impossible to carry
all one's weight

     impossible to justify this life,
     earth I stand on, air I breathe,
     clear water plunging
     of its own weight
     into my cup.

     I can't carry much—
     a full canteen's too heavy
     but a spring-fed stream in every canyon
     meets my thirst

what is given    not solely limitation
but abundance:
more gifts than we can drink in.

     Under these stony peaks
     reservoirs go on collecting,
     burst out most brightly
     from the narrowest fissures

(v)

Rock under my foot
takes on that 33-pound pack
till my legs are extruded granite

I no longer carry this load
but the rock—
                    pillars that pass downward
inward through the earth's caves and rivers
to the molten center.

        Now it is fire
that effortlessly bears the burden

(vi)

More technical advice:
        in packing your knapsack
        place the heaviest items on top.

        Shoulder these, keep them
        uppermost in your mind,

        knottiest problems
        where your greatest strength is.

        Buckle the frame's webstrap
        across your pelvis—
        weight shifts to that point

        but every woman knows this

(vii)

Burden of the body:
        because of it
        loitering street bums
        hiss out their hatred

I am my body.
>Impossible to say:
>*it* is what
>they hate

I am who they hate:
>being alone
>"resolved to call
>no man master"

burden of the body's history:
>the man's blundering entry
>the birth-tearing
>submitted to

as if owed, and not a gift given.

I carry this weight
>whether I want to or not
>naked into the arms
>of my lover

who trembles the deeper he enters.

>He learns my body's power.
>It is not his.
>He cannot touch it.

I carry my self
>alone all night
>up a steep trail

among rocks
>the lair of the rattlesnake
>and the mauling bear,

carry my weight

beyond delusions of support.
No one else
         can smooth my path
or clothe me in sunny weather.

No moon:
the air is cold.

The lean cheekbone meets it.

## IX.  MOUNTAIN DEATH-CAMAS

*hiking the Phantom Terrace trail*

(i)

In marshy shade
masses of ivory bells

splinters of the moon
around a gold star-center

root, stem, leaf, flower
all fatal

(ii)

in sun mirrored
off a glacial lake

a young man

sleeps on grass
hair moon-pale

unprotected face
reddening to purple

I should wake him

warn against the sun—
at these cool heights

we forget
it burns

(iii)

Not my problem,
this man who doesn't
know the mountains.

He's brought a ten-speed bike
new, emerald and chrome
to 12,000 feet—

must have had to carry
what was meant
to carry him.

Bright technological sun
unquestioned,
we never look at you.

We say we see
by you
even when blinded

(iv)

Warrior sun—the winner!

cannon to blast the moon
out of the sky.

I protect myself

with hat, dark glasses,
long-sleeved shirt

rely on feet

to carry me past
the camas-laden meadow

and the sleeper

past tree-line
where the path disappears.

Rocks only now

      and boots resisting

       (v)

I walk into the moon's country.
Her fullness rises,
a cooled and softened sun.

Both eyes of the sky
have cleared, strip
down to essential body,

lose the flesh of thought.
My white bones float
out to meet that naked source

by which I see both dark and light,
wildflower both beautiful
and lethal—
         no illusion

therefore no consolation

       (vi)

Daylight:

down again to the clouded lake,
the meadow ambiguously starry

to hear he'd killed himself
—the youth with moon-pale hair—

and boy scouts found
beside his shattered skull

a pistol new and silver
as his ten-speed racer.

                    Ah.

                              Inexplicable loss, that life
consumed by its own terror

not mine—
          I have three sons

one dark, two fair
who ask which boots are best,

which packframe lifts the load.

They also need my words,
can only hear

their own

               (vii)

Cortège of motorcycles
bears away
the messy body-remnant

leaving tire-tracks
in the crushed camas.

The web of death
hangs everywhere
not mine to weave

or to untangle.
In it that pale hair

is twined with mine.
Choiceless I choose
the moon

as two in one.
And deeper shadows form

under the edge illumined.

# Climbing Uncompaghre

*13,000 feet in the San Juan
mountains with Patrick, age 15*

A side trail down
as if to water
but the creek is dry—

no path beyond: we think
we'll find it later,
come instead to bones

a deer's bleached ribcage.
A sad place, my son says.
Bare rock-cliff facing us

we've missed our way:
we backtrack, climb
the ridge and see our path again

stamped into deep grasses.

Not our last sadness:
the winter I left, he came
to visit, wrote on my tenement desk

"I cried for my mom and me."
We ate Christmas dinner on the floor;
we had no table.

Now in our summer hiking
still we carry loads
on our backs, and trailfood.

My son says, look at the stream
running from the peak

and I say where? where?

He says, we'll make it.
Above, a thin scar of path
crosses the mountain's shoulder

to the base
of that gray rock-tower
where the last scaling starts.

# Correspondences

*September in the Colorado Rockies*

When red stars glow ruddier—Antares a ruby
in the scorpion's armor, Arcturus a copper eye—
look along the ground for crimson leaves replying:
five-pointed wild geranium, grape holly, strawberry
leaf fruit and tendril. Look at your own hands
chapped in the first frost, and the campfire dying.

# Rosita Cemetery

(i)

Graveyards
are stiller
than other hillsides

They hold
nothing
but the attempt to hold

Plastic wreaths
are sadder
in their lasting

than an obelisk
with a name.

(ii)

In stillness here
vitality

out of hard ground:
the mind leaps

invents these dead
as if their histories

seethe on
hidden under gravestones:

wind always stirs
this plot of pines

beyond them
walls of heat immobile,

boulder
in a dry creekbed.

Even in that fixity

a lizard

darts into shadow.

# Gentians

*near the Sangré de Cristos,*
*after the accidental death*
*of Robert Secora, 17*

A purple gash
in the oat fields' wide green
spread out below still-snowy mountains—

Barbed wire blocks us:
gingerly I lower it
for the ranch foreman's wife to step over.

We wade across
to gaze down into the fringed cups
lit, it seems, by the earth's dark blood.

She tells me how
they had to send away the homeless boy
who later fell under the blade at Canda's sawmill—

the ranch's owner
wouldn't take him in
so how could they? She says

"Did you ever see
so many gentians? I used to find just one
or two. We might as well pick plenty—

tomorrow they cut
these oats—see, the kernel's
just coming out of the splitting pod—"

# Fireweed

In the charred clearing
fireweed

which won't seed
in undamaged turf

proliferates.

Pinkish-purple tongues
of flame leap into the air

where one midsummer night
the campground dump burned,

its glow the only light
on the mountain.

We rode up by jeep,
kept watch a long time

lest the blaze take
the whole forest—

covertly pleased by
danger and the finality

of that consumption.

# Locoweed

When cattle eat it
they go mad and die—but we

find it *mille fleurs* in a meadow,
spikes of streaked white-lavender

or shading blue to purple,
tall candles in the grass

we gather by the armload
splendid as the mountain air

that also shades from blue
to purple, clouds in it mauve-white

scudding and billowing—
great space in motion,

dome of high lucidity
calm in its lunatic hues

over us. And beside us
locoweed stabs and glows

in a blue bowl on the windowsill.

# Western Gothic Romantic Classic

Moonlight slips a white knifeblade
inside the tepee door.

The ground is hard and the man
whose lean hipbones hook with hers

is a stranger—mountain climber
he said, first ascent in the Andes,

cited *Jefe* he said, Peace Corps, strumming
guitar by the campfire where she stumbled in

after a lonely hitch in the badlands
and the black hills. She's thirsty.

Who asks where water comes from
after a long drought? She drinks all night

from his fountain and he from hers.
He ropes her to his piton and she falls free.

At 3 a.m. she dreams him as Orion
climbing the eastern sky with a sword of stars.

At dawn they wake and laugh; they're caked
with dirt they beat out of the old sleeping bag.

He asks her to stay, to ride and climb
with him, and she says yes.

Through desert sage and rock they walk
back to the ranch house. Dry country.

Rattlesnakes, she thinks. One thin trickle
piped into the horse corral.

Inside after stark sunlight
it's hard to see—

cougar and bearskin on the bed,

.44 magnum and ammunition belt

slung on the bedpost.
From a photo he is smiling

leaning on a rifle
wearing a green beret.

# At Midmonth

Ripening in my darkness
every month

not a red moon to reduce me
to useful function

nor a wound to stopper
with bandages

—I say a woman is not a myth
not an emergency ward

not an empty cup to be filled
blest—

it thickens    one silk layer quilted
over another

a fine soft place    our warmth
the child-bed

every man wants to be brought to.
But you know

ripeness is not all    is stasis
binds

bursts    unable to ask
the next question:

time then to undo
throw away

bits of string   clips   bands
the lump of petrified wood

in the desk drawer    everything
we save

thinking someday it may save us,
slough off

with only a slight pang
all those prized sentiments

and start over. I'm glad to move
into another house

carpeting   curtaining—a chance
to "make it new."

Just as glad to say goodbye
to a lover,

pack a knapsack, move on.

So at mid-month    I pitch my tent
in a deep valley,

listen to its rivers
underground:

new blood rising
to feed

to shed.

# After Yeats

Take care, he said, your poems are almost
too beautiful (he who often makes too much
of her "beauty"). Under lovely images pain is lost
or blunted—do you want that, he asked.

                                                   She's tough,
she thinks, and unromantic, sworn to accost
her self-deception, but is re-reading Yeats—mistake—
and loves his elegance, wants to bypass pain and sing
a desert world in music golden and piercing.

(ii)

Under noon sun someone rides a white mare
down from the mountains, through boulders and pine.
She's wearing jeans and a green halter, with bare
brown back and shoulders, midriff lean
from pitching hay. Her hat falls back and frees her hair.
Her lover, almost ex-, dismounted, watches. Two men
walk to her stirrup, offer up a coffee-can
of wild raspberries. She scoops a handful,

raises it red and dripping till the juice
runs down her arm. Slowly she licks
the fruit-blood off her skin. Her hair blows into
her mouth. Red smears her lips.
Throned in the saddle she sits sensuously
eating, and the men look down, abashed by this.
The horse stands and shakes the loose reins
while rubies splash onto her snowy mane.

# A Bracelet of Turquoise from Aguilar

On my arm, three small oceans
anchored on two silver equators,

their green-blue brilliant as mountain noon,
ecstatic hue, the shimmer of a glacial lake

two thousand feet below the climber
who walks the highest ledge over sheer drop

not perfectly steady but facing
both heights and depths, luminous herself

in that blue luminosity.

Turquoise from Aguilar contains black matrix.
A heavy continent upthrust blots out the blue,

outlines it.
            I walk, in a nightmare, a tunnel
or half-blind street, searching how to

"clean up my act." A woman friend is angry:
you were rude, you were reading when you should

have been watching the actors—her eyes
are light blue.
             I wake to strange knowledge.

In waking life she likes me, especially for
not hiding how I build myself up, how I strive

for those heights and expansions. In this waking
the man who loves me holds me in his arms.

That dark weight I call my "self" heaves up
rough-edged into turquoise air, the opening day.

The dream-self fades, the day-self won't resume,
too tentative, yet both are lingering—

On my arm, the weight of this rock: blue

waters, black islands sand-polished to luster,

poise in the grip of bright metal that's hammered
and beaten and molded.
                                        The sky

opens endlessly outward but never
fails to encircle the planet.

# ◄ PART II ►
## *On Loss*

# Anti-Cycle for the New Year

(i)

Dark days,
    thin snow on the roofs.

Graying, he described me.

    Too long a mother:

        no cycle
of return to
    before that.

(ii)

Light snow on the airfield
    —take it lightly.

The great engines grind,

    lift my sons off
        our common ground

    in a long curve
        opening.

(iii)

Poets praise motherhood
    especially
    if they are fathers
and move on to
    less burdened women.

> No new start for me,
> only the old
effort to juggle loss
> against
> the continual gift
>
> wrapped in tissue
> that gets thrown away.

(iv)

I strip the tree whose little lights
the shivering tinsel multiplied —
hopes, joys —

When I was a child I thought I'd die
after Christmas. I thought rightly:
nothing ahead but comedown.

I lit a tree for my sons, who fly
east, who will wing back my way,
but it's not my symbol,

this cut convention drying in a corner,
seduction clung to —
now I lean
towards plain day. I stand

at its uncurtained window.

(v)

Pity these cycles
beginning again:

the woman betrayed by lovers
will once more encounter brutes;
connoisseurs who find little to suit
their tastes will find less;

the writer of radical protest
will find the middle class more obtuse;
the taciturn poet at parties
will find the girls mute —

all will come beg me to tell them
they're right because they are wronged

and my cycle starts. I'll be drawn
into murmuring sympathy — yes,
I support your plausible lie:
external forces exist
and are vicious —

         Again I'll be drawn
into failing to say what I know,
what I constantly say to myself
as a charm against panic:

> *The world's self-made.*
> *Observe! Observe!*

    (vi)

The long curve of the year
      empties.

We're out of bread:
      must get more
      somewhere.

Supplies come through
      on odd timetables.

We rotate on a bent
      axle-tree
      —thus the Sahara
         once a polar icecap.

You can see the bend itself
         on the non-stop jet
         to California,

the mind in its long passage
                  over the winter Rockies

         its momentary lights
              a pattern
              on the night airfield:
         gray snow

         going back to water.

# Mayday and All

*for Jeff, born in May*

"Nothing is so beautiful
as spring,"
says Hopkins.

Elizabeth Bishop writes:
the cow takes
a long time

eating her calf's after-birth.
I'm not
as driven as before

this May morning—
don't get to
Inwood School till 9:20.

Children write poems
under my direction,
puzzle out

the ways of symbolizing.
I'm pleased     relaxed
lean back against the black-

board—
        suffering floods me
and last night's dream:

        I was menstruating
        huge clots—my liver
        guts, spleen

came away and lay
thick in a basin where
my son (who'll be 18

tomorrow) looked and touched them.

Again
a downward pressure
in my body.

I woke thinking:

more
is coming away.

# My Father's Death

(i)

Under the long lanai
I weed out parched ferns

from among the green.

The fern-bed grows in the humus
of a great oak's stump.

Years ago my father

left a space in the new roof
to frame that tree.

Now an empty square
lets in

the sky beyond it.

(ii)

Sun everywhere
hammers gold on every leaf-edge—

laurel, buckeye, jasmine.
Grapevines open a green fan

over the birdfeeder.
Jays fly down

find no seed    dry waterdish
binoculars in a closed case

on the redwood table.

(iii)

No body:
that unimaginable change—

to be in my own body

is painful

a pull on it
a tearing away

of the root.


Yet grass that bent under his foot
a few days ago

still bends to the wind,
rebounds.

                    The sun
on new-leafing oaks

must hold a part of him
burning in the air,

a body-house
for my intensest longing.

                    (iv)

Here droop roses, Paul Scarlets
my father trellised in the buckeye
purpling as they fade

last week as rich as blood,
as velvet—a touch of human art
in the random green

like the garnet pendants he bought
for my mother's ears,
or carnation stuck in his lapel.

In the lanai's vines once he hid
a clay owl-bell,
music to answer the linnets.

      Everywhere in this garden
my father's touch:
I can't bring myself

to prune the roses    must watch
every petal dry and fall

each rosehip shrivel

to a knobbed bone.

      (v)

Dream:

in a suit of cream-colored linen
he comes walking

I seize his white hand:

"I know you're dead
but how good to touch

even a vision"

      (vi)

All that's left of my father's body:
my body

that speaks the book of the dead
to itself:

*Whatever you see, however terrifying,*
        *recognize*

        *as your own radiant mind—*

my father's mind

living in me    windborne red-throated bird
that flies

between light and no-light.
                    The space
is empty.

It is what I see. Pain radiates.
In its broken flame

he lives.

# On Loss: Five Meditations

*for A.J.M*

(i)

## *Meditation on the Void*

"Gone, gone
gone beyond—"

mantra misunderstood
as deprivation

terror of losing
familiar pain

as if dying—
no heart, if no ache—

my loss!
my loss!

but my cry finds
no wave to carry it

(ii)

## *Dealing with Guilt*

A false note
in this suffering:
as if

touching
the ark of the Lord
I'm killed for it,

the child in me
battered by stones
under the fathers' law:

in me
the mother wakes
and speaks gently

to that child:

you are not
bearer of the world
like God.

No blame.

*(iii)*

*On Change*

Remember the star
at the tip of summer's tentpole

gone now
behind the white mountain?

We cannot remember
what is always here

.   .   .

But I remember you
as if unchanged.

The error hurts.
We're not selves

fixed in orbit
but elements decaying.

.   .   .

After that star explodes
its light
will reach us for a while.

Two truths in one—
it burns
and is burned out.

Change
is our only continuity.

(iv)

*After the Winter Solstice*

Out of a dark season
sun turns
imperceptibly towards us,

candle taller
the longer it's lit:
light in the mind

rising
earlier,
reaches deeper

into thickest
sharp-needled pine
this little

then
a little more:
the way

coming into the world

.   .   .

and coming into myself
that slowly—
not seeing

at first:
stung and meshed
in my own

dark branches
but
waking every morning

to look
out of a window
slightly less gray.

(v)

*Meditation on Endings*

In a German prison
the condemned man marvels

      at a laurel leaf
floating in his soup

         "its tracery of veins,
          its perfect form."

Between us    bars after all,
the last visit made

       ·  ·  ·

Let it be executed.

Let me be
restored
to the branch in leaf.

# Masque: Apparitions Out of the Life of Fiona Starker

*huerfano, Sp., orphan*
*scene: southern Colorado*


## I. ANTE-MASQUE

In the mountains, no mothers.
        Huerfano's a desert county
        and I live north of it

but I don't need to be held
        or rocked. I stoke my own cabin stove
        with pine, warm up enough

till Fiona Starker with her russet hair
        rides by on her Texas palomino.
        I follow and bow to her

on the stone doorstep of Phantom Ranch,
        a woman my mother's age
        who is alone

with husband, horses, money in oil
        and souvenirs of travel. We talk
        all night of journeys,

passages unseen and seen. I tell her:
        the moon is my mother
        who lights the mountain's tip.

She says: the night is mine,
        whose chill makes me build
        so big a fire.

I say: your hair itself is fiery.
       Listen, she says, to the tongues
of flame:


## II.  Masque: Apparitions


              (i)

*Limousine*

I am driving too fast along a desert track
at shadowless noon
              in my scarlet sports car, a Triumph
              bought to blot out the death of my son—
                     driving away from his ashes
                     buried near Rosita, the ghost town,
driving west to the Sangré de Cristos
toward Phantom Ranch where I live alone
(my husband off in oilfields somewhere)

ahead of me I see a black Cadillac
limousine, in it
              two priests with grim faces fixed
              on the mountains and the abbot's
                     retreat house, my only neighbor.
                     I pass them, speeding.
Why don't they turn their head to look at me?
My hair blows and blazes like copper;
my steering hand is ringed with tiger's-eye.

I glance in the rearview mirror. Dust billows
and clears. The road
              is empty. No priests, no limousine.
              I stop, get out. For fifty miles, clean
                     to the Spanish Peaks—emptiness.

              Meeting the abbot next week
in town, I ask half-joking if he lost two priests

on the road to Phantom Ranch. He glares
and turns away.

At nightfall I sit at solitaire.
Lightning burns moonwhite
          among the piñons. The cards speak
          of two black kings, messengers
                    of forces that can bend a life
                    to ashes and send a woman out
into desperate places.
                              But my speeding sports car
has conjured them away, my red Triumph
that sees these apparitions but will not give in.

          (ii)

*The Thimble*

All day I hunt my new brass thimble
          in bureau drawers,
          jewel-boxes

          while maple leaves press their gold palms
          against the leaded
          windows—

                    cold wind through New Jersey woods
                              where Washington's men
executed
          one of their own, a traitor.

Dry vines rattle on the grape arbor
          where my eight-year-old son sat
          in his wheelchair

          before I had to leave him
          in the hospital
          too long ago

to think of—I traveled then,
                    Paris, Milan, Beirut...

Tonight, no button
                    on my winter coat, no way to sew it.

            .   .   .

Alone in the house I sleep.
            At dawn on the bedside table
            a thimble

            fluted silver, such as a woman
            might have used
            in 1775
                    says to me:
                            mend—
                            mend—

but vine leaves
                    have been embroidered
green on linen;
            gold cannot be stitched to lawns.
            The fabric of the past
            is seamless.

            At twenty-two he chose
            to end his wheelchair life—

                    Why
                            do you send a tool
too late?

I had no choice.

            .   .   .

Now, alone in the western mountains
I hang up larkspur,

monkshood

to dry, flowers for winter.
The brittle stems
whisper

in the cellar.
                          I sleep.
And rise to find
the silver thimble

on the rose-pink rim
of the washstand.

                 (iii)

*A Winter's Night*

Blizzard builds a wall
              against my storm doors.
Fire burns hotly
              behind its screen
Snow falls again,
                 the road
   to Phantom Ranch impassable.

Snowed in two miles away
              that catty woman telephones:
a mountain lion's down
              prowling her pasture,
our minister's wife is
                 divorcing him,
   says he beats her—

I hang up. Silence
              outside silence.
I never spoke in court, for
              the child's sake
                 though I could have told

                          the judge plenty.
    Diamonds

replaced tears. I bought expensive
            Paris silks, a blouse
richly crocheted, white
            to start over in,
bride to myself alone—
                          Are the doors locked?
    The mountain lion

tracks down the loner or
            the winter-weakened,
travels fifty miles a night
            as fast as gossip.
Well, the altar silver's tarnished
                      and the lode
    has petered out.

What then the worth of death
            and silence?

This new husband that I can't
            live with nor
live without, who's gone
            again—
                          but hush!
I rise, make tea, play
                  solitaire.
    My sleep is hard

and blank. Pale morning finds
            snow over all untouched
but my bedroom closets open.
            The white silk blouse
is dangling from its cushioned hanger
                      ripped to shreds
    as if by cat's claws.

# Nightsong For Two Voices

*(i)*

*for C. and M.*

## Song of the Brain-Damaged Girl

i am a rocking chair
down and up    down and up
air is blinking
sometimes i am a creek
loose over stones
splash comes back and back
my cold toes sing
to my cold fingers

some nights i am the cat
holding in secrets
i am her quiet corner
and orange slit eyes
dishes rattling    my mother's voice
makes things happen
cat weaves under the rocker
listening to air

when no one's talking i'm afraid
i'll disappear
i try to wake my ears
i try to stop it
water erasing
a blackboard—
shapes like sleep
pushing up
in my throat...

## Song of Her Mother In Reply

You are my midnight puzzle-piece.
Wakeful I turn
and turn you again to fit
into the green garden of my living.
But you obtrude.

The mower's blade flings up
a stone that blinds me.
My fingers cannot bring you to flower.

Yet this morning I watch you
rocking under the pines.
The sun is good to you;
cat sleeps in your hands.
You feel what we all feel
and your kindness draws out mine.
Now I root myself
beside you deep in human ground.

        .  .  .

But your eyes close before they close.
A tornado tears into the trees.
I look at you, mirror
of my mind edging blackness,
shapes pushing up—
Then I can only reach out, reach in
to whatever will hold us all,
my daughter, the terror,
insoluble love and pain.

# Dry Season

*visiting California*

A long drought, but outside my mother's windows
green of oak, acacia, laurel
    conceals the hardening soil

My bachelor brother stammers, comes home every
weekend. Old streetcars his one hobby,
    on Saturdays he lays trolley-

track for a rail museum up the hot valley.
He is a perfect son, echoes the phrases
    his late father spoke, unlike me never rages

or weeps. The lawn browns only in patches.
We look at the pines, don't notice withered
    buckeyes. Radio says "perfect weather"

meaning: no rain, when rain is all that's needed.
Yet this week desert thunderstorms in Mexico
    drowned hundreds. I watched my brother mow

what lawn is left. He said, "We used to vacuum
up the cuttings. Now we let the grass
    grow through." Over the past

three days I've seen
that green absorb its dead.
    And in woods behind it the brown spreads.

# Cragmont Avenue Childhood

(i)

*Windows*

I looked north from my bedroom window
into thick pines and acacias.
I wanted to climb out by a rope,
become an explorer in that
tangled forest.

From my bedroom's west window
I saw the bay, a blue platter
on bright days. I wanted
white sails to skim out through
the Golden Gate

under my own power, like gull's wings,
like wind, irrepressible.
I wanted to cross illegally
into unkempt gardens adjoining mine
where goldfish slept

in the depths of a rocky pool
and surfaced, glittering.
I wanted my own garden,
hedged, in it narcissi and
thornless roses.

I sat in my own white bedroom
on my ruffled and spotless bed.

*Sandbox*

Stepping out of the french doors
into the patio hot
under my barefoot sandals

stepping over the splintery high
blue sides of the sandbox
into the warm grainy

half-pleasant uncertain sand—
I might have been climbing
mountains, it was that

adventuresome. All morning
I staggered in that small sea
while bees whirred overhead

in honeysuckle. I staggered
and stood, bent, sat. Sand
grated everywhere, sticking

to my body. It was not nice
exactly—it was like dirt
maybe, but playful. I loaded

and unloaded buckets of sand
and nothing much was happening,
it seemed.

## The Basement

Possessions hoarded in orange crates:
nails and tools to patch, repair, align—

Down dark stairs to the "drying room":
my undershirts pinned on lines strung up

over trunks stuffed with my mother's
and grandmother's raiment:

I dressed up, pledged myself that someday
I'd wear velvet and bugle-beads

with no musty smell. I changed to jeans,
crawled under the foundations

on hands & knees through the black cave
around and down to the garage:

I opened every door in that basement—
paint closet, furnace room, old victrola—

I inspected all the things we owned
believing that they held what I could know,

believed it after I left home
and my parents cleaned out the house for tenants:

I still go down those stairs
rifling through cans of missing & broken parts

trying to name their blind odors.

# I Help My Mother
# Move Out of Her Old House
# in the Napa Valley

(i)

It is not my life
under these lichened oaks,
   these redwood eaves
but my mother's life—

I was ten and climbed
a young laurel where she couldn't
   see me, and laurel leaves
touched my hair with pungent fingers.

She called and I came
back, and didn't mess up
   paper with my writing.
I followed her housework

inside stone walls.
Outside the rich stink of sun
   on grass and poison oak—
Sleeping nights under an unfinished roof

I covered my head
as a bat's wing
   fanned me in the dark.

(ii)

The house is a body
from which we come;
   now it is emptying out.

Is it her life only
        that disappears as I am
packing, filing, discarding?

My mother sits in the bath
        massaging cramped legs,
in place of her left breast

the skin pinned neat and flat
        across, under it the heart
pulsing.

In the pale water,

        slightly distorted,
her ankles, blue with burst veins

are slender as mine.

        *(iii)*

Paintings done when I was eighteen,
        twenty-two, mementos of talent—
no room for them in
        my makeshift apartment,
nor for my father's book of Schubert's songs,

but I take these: *vom Wasser*
        *haben wir's gelernt*
how to move on—
        maybe I'll sing yet.
Rain falls these nights

in dusty California. I sit up
        late and listen to the dripping.
Old papers in the garage await
        our junkman.
In the morning my mother

greets me in her green pants-suit.
  Buds tip the laurels.
I wrap and mail to myself
    her old evening gowns.

We will never leave this place.

# The Stars

(i)

In the mind's midnight
the fixed stars ride

tonight I gaze at the space
between them

(ii)

A ruddy star invisible
until it falls

and then for a moment
flaring

I long to see it stay
—a comet, a signal—

but only its exploding gave it
that luminous trail

of fire

(iii)

At midnight
two darknesses:

confusion
and illimitable space—

in the west
a star-sickle to slash through;

overhead the dipper
swings from Arcturus's peg

pours out what it
cannot contain

what does not
contain it

(iv)

In the northeast burns
Yellow-white Capella
star of the first magnitude

in the meadow grass
its slow imitator
ignites    goes out    goes on

(v)

The stars live in the dark
as I do

I lie down on the bony ground
to stare up

letting go—

O diamonds, fall into my eyes
become my seeing

clear and indestructible.

## ❦ PART III ❧

# *Reclamations*

# By Night

Moon-sliver: darkness rises
to hone its edge.
Our love as soon as we spoke it
entered nightfall.
We hold hands on the road
and cold wind chills them.

A star fell, you tell me
but I wasn't looking.

> *I'm alone. The stars see nothing*
> *but I stare back, design their meaning*
> *as a jeweler sets diamonds:*
> *the scorpion has stung me,*
> *the archer draws his bow*
> *to pierce me—*

Last sun-trace gone, no road. We stumble
over rocks. Why
did you do that? What
did you mean? Words
into darkness, our hands clench.
Sky only slightly lighter than massed pines
is slashed by the moon's curved sword,
heart's weapon, crescent phase.

(ii)

Crowned by the deathless stars, imagining
one won't die, yet they speed outward, losing us—
Antares, "opposing Mars," that blood-soaked planet,
also is red, roils in its ruby gases, dying.

That jeweled wound throbs all night.

In empty dark death reddens,
 swallows me. I burn to blackness,
crowned with bone.

Enter this open torture.

Take this charred hand and come.

# A Self-Portrait Fails

(i)

A self-portrait fails
from intense effort not to beautify,
refusal to shy away
from any flaw.
>    But black pen-line's too blunt
>    for shadows' subtleties.
Hopeless to shape hair's mass
>    filament by filament,
>    though nothing less is truthful—

Five Matissean strokes might do it better
but cheat on the harder questions.
Anxious honesty
ticks in each fine point
>    ("you over-explain," says a friend)
>    derange the whole.
Low forehead can't be erased
>    back to its plain height—
>    the image over-pretty after all:
too much romantic blackening.

(ii)

But why a mirror anyway and self as subject?
Better the outward apples of Cézanne, objective eye,
>                    the world
>    compassionately studied.

On the desk, cluttered with the world's requests,
a mess, I wanted to set a glass
>            prop up
>    the artist's pad beside

that imaged face and try to build the infra-structure,
the illusory "very thing itself."

                If the hand
          can link to thought,

then form  externalized in black on white
cements belief.
                      What's wanted
is a stronger replica

to stare back from the page, immutable
and reassuring: yes, this is—
                    this is more
          than vaporous assemblage

          and moment of its failing.

# Cold Flashes

*Redwood Canyon, California*

More cold than hot,
these irrelevant shivers of body-change—
a warning, the first frost.
                    One might

walk out in such an autumn dawn
under the leafless branch of the persimmon
gazing at that bright fruit, and say: now

it is ripe, frost-nipped; no fever here
and no distortion. But eating the persimmon
makes the mouth pucker from the tart edge

of the scraped skin. Pain without dignity
don't mention it—a flush freezes under
my shirtsleeves. The monthly bleeding had

meant renewal. Now the moon is locked behind
low fog. I walk in a mist of silver,
shattered droplets of the moon. This back road

narrows past vineyards, past our stonewalled
country house, now sold, and deadends
up the hill somewhere. I wanted change

not to be so radical. Prune trees were uprooted
to plant these vines, an axe to white spring
blossoming. What ripens now? The grapevines too

are bare. I'm haunted. Nothing certain
in this travel, no road signs, yet everywhere
deep smells of leaf-mould under redwoods,

*sequoia sempervirens,* the after-perfume
of dissolving forms. Not much to count on.
Thought in its soft reflections echoes moonlight

drifts and holds its own.

# For Buddhist Friends
# on the Birth of their Twins

*She is the treasure of the house.*
*Great good fortune.*
                        —I Ching

### (i)

A white bird rises over a mountain trail,
her wing star-pale
against thick pine branches.

In the grass a leaf-mottled
brown bird startles:
            rustle of wings, a bright eye.

### (ii)

Anna is grace and power,
beneficence of your broken heart.
Whenever you walk by moonlight
you will think: she, infinite pearl,
            mirror of the sun
but purer, as tears are purer than water.

### (iii)

A third son is magic.
Disinherited in fairytales,

where the first son becomes king,
second son his general,

what left for the third but seeking?

He slips out alone by dark
penniless, homeless, to find

he can leap the river of poison
fly over the double ring of snow peaks
to the source—Michaël,
      warrior-prince,
      "who is like god?"

       (iv)

Great good fortune, this birth-journey.
Cloud-moving wind
leads us to take the narrow road
to the deep north.

         Bashō:
     "in the utter silence of a temple,
     a cicada's voice alone
     penetrates the rocks."

# Waking in Front of a Cracked Mirror

This jagged life
holds at the frame's edges

but the body fractures in the center
of the glass I salvaged

off the street,
hung over our loft-bed

to increase light in close quarters.
This body

disjointed at breast
and breast-bone, subject

to chills and sweats, matches
this mind caught

in bifurcations,
inconsistencies. Look, voyeur of self,

and laugh at this cubist nude,
a patchy image

the only possible reflection of fact.

Next to the cracked mirror
a branch of bittersweet

has stood
through two winters and still offers

its gnarled orange fruit. The background's
dark, the figure shifty.

A life torn apart under this dual
emblem—the seed's

endurance and the easy
shatter of gleaming surfaces.

Before the mirror was hung, the wall
showed cracked as well,

and grimy. Can't
redecorate my life, its pain

and spackle over every defect,
can't

choose what stays or leaves:
I sleep badly
                fragmented

            .   .   .

Dawn opens naturally behind the curtains.
Sun doubles

in the glass.
My thoughts, your thoughts, pale scraps split,

bodies float and re-assemble in the
morning light

                    rise

in that riven silver.

# Autumn Meditation

*for my daughter on her 24th birthday*

October dusk: we're walking east on 60th street.

As many years of my life have passed
since your birth as before it—
from now on I am clearly more mother than child.

Dry leaves blow from planetrees onto stoops
of brownstones. You, my autumn daughter, in russet
blouse and fawn-beige skirt, stride beside me

firmly, as if I were in your charge, might go
astray. Apparently I've given you my strengths
and certainties, left myself with questions,

ruminations which seem to you too fragile,
remnants of oak and maple. Leaves swirl around us,
making the fall wind's power visible. Secretly

I still want to teach you, not how to master the world
any more, but how to trust it, let its beauty happen.
Tomorrow you fly back to Paris. Now we stand

on this broken leaf-strewn curb, a balance-point,
your birthday, when I came to life as your mother,
and you, strong as now in your first push outward,

took on the burden of my courage that lets you go.

# For Patrick, My Son

(i)

About the divorce
      my incomprehensible explanations
      over airport salad
          "it's certain that fine women eat /
      a crazy salad with their meat"
*that* I understood—but

didn't want
      to eat crazy    or be fine
      I think he thought… but you know
         it must be night
      for the moon to rise,
that calm mind which sees itself

chopped to bits on the riffled lake.

      If I say I feared I wasn't sane
you'll be afraid    but
         if I was
      then why—?   But night falls
every night: we sit
to eat. In the chef's salad sliced cheese
      and ham, no more strange a mix
         than any other. Bit by bit
we take it in

(ii)

In the play the deaf girl's
      only speech is weeping:
         that we understood
      without a translator

but within limits: her sign language
        lucid  to those
        who know it, gate to meaning

In a prickly barberry bush
        beside my office
                bird-whistles, chortlings,
        no visible sign of their source—
the deaf girl's hand
        gestures invisible thread
        from her heart to his

incomplete
        need
                help
        "This isn't the place to talk,
—we can't," you say
        my fork by your fork shredding the lettuce.

# Reclamation: Aspen Stump and Willow

*a watercolor in the Colorado mountains*

Aspen stump and willow:
new green out of gray—
this mountain's strewn with silvered logs
brought down by years of snow and beavers.
      So what one remembers
          lies cumbersome but tarnishing,
    loses its sharp edges.
Around it spring new grass tufts,
aspen lemon-green, blue spruce,
white violets and arrowleaf,
altering that landscape.
      Old logs locked into a curved dam
         make a new lake;
    old creek trickle leaps this year
in white waterfalls.
This new husband tries fishing
with my dead father's flyrod.
Each night he looks up, says
    the skies are clearer,
      the Milky Way starrier
than the night before.

# Any Mother's Unsent Letters

(i)

*to a son in the midwest from back east*

A clipped azalea twig unwatered since autumn
blooms a pink frill by the frost-rimmed window.

I teach poem-writing to squirmy tenth grade boys.
Marginalia: "This poet sucks." It's Friday. Your

anger too lurks cheerfully. Nightmare of loss recurred
but my car, not my purse, was stolen. Hunting

for money to buy it back, I overslept, drove up island
to the high school, slow truck in front, red van tailgating.

Not so late after all. I pay big phone bills.
You say you'll go back to college at the vernal equinox.

(ii)

*to a son down south from up north*

In my study a whole wall bulges with books. Computer's
cursor swiftly ticks lines out of a bursting mind.

I write, you write: how does poetry make politics?
You are a political journal's El Salvador expert.

*Salvator* is masculine. A mother's mistakes comprise
many pages of X-ed out facts, insurrections.

American mayhem—divorce. Blood all over. The boy
tells the counselor "I know my mom will always love me."

For your wedding in May I'll buy the bouquets and corsages.
Outside, snow sinks between hummocks of half-green grass.

(iii)

*to a son in the far west, more or less*

Short takes: fear-flashbulbs explode in the dark. Booze.
Bars. Gay guy's taunt. Fight. In dirty snow his wallet tossed

(they said) by you. Blank. Jail. No memory, no defense.
Workhouse months in fear-safety. Out, out…these things pass.

Taxi driving. Fare after fare accrues merit. No drinks.
New girl deserts. Bills. Back at school graphics training

goes slow. Each hand-inked letter must perfectly stay
within bounds. How long since we walked in clear mountain air

among pines where a wild creek's water-leaps and pools
made us speak together of all things' ever-living goodness?

(iv)

*to a daughter who lives abroad*

Slim in a fire-pink batik dress beside the pea-green parrot
of Sainte-Phalle's fountain, you never strive for impact.

You step onto the music-barge *La Péniche* at Pont St-Michel,
fumble for cigarettes. From below, African drums reverberate.

Your voice on Sunday radio *sur la mort d'un algérien
tué dans les rues* simply requests justice, an end to racism.

Rue Notre-Dame de Nazareth, birthplace of Otto Diesel,
with penthouse chandeliers and rose gardens—what's relevant?

Murmurs: oh mother don't… Dusk on the Seine. Late sun gilds
cathedral towers. You look up, skeptical, elegant, aloof.

(v)

*to the stepson who comes on weekends*

McDonald's, Adidas, Izod, Newcleus, Haagen-Daz, Kiss
Def Leppard, Police, The Terminator, VCR, Star Trek, Star Wars

J.H.S. 184, M-15 bus up First, M-14 crosstown, Frank's
Pizzeria, Pepsi, M & Ms, anywhere after school but homework.

Quarters for PacMan, Alligators, Bombs Away—the brain beeps
digitally, chasing orange and green dayglo blobs all night.

Age of innocence. Your crammed skull makes Calcutta's streets
look like denuded prairie. I'm out of it, finding no way

to hawk what has no brand name. I hardly blame you.
Why shouldn't you have these airbags to cushion the crash?

## ◄ PART IV ►

# *What Is Coming*

# Dislocations

*in memoriam Richard Borden*
*from East Hampton, New York*

Yesterday a bobwhite dropped down on the corner deck rail,
rust-stained feathers ruffled and bent by late wind.
Black and white stripes curved his head with surety.
My gaze steadied him. But fidgety I turned to tune
radio's jazz to softer classical—and he was gone.
Wood birds don't find enough seed here: my fault.

Again the lost purse nightmare, my San Andreas fault-
line, where deep earth-shifts begin. I wake and rail
against myself. I've lost my keys. No dream: they're gone,
as long ago my friend Anne lost the carpool-van keys. Wind
blows friends away. "Time like an everlasting—" Hymn tune
forgotten pricks green in winter-blanched lawn's surety.

NASA loses its Delta rocket. Red Chernobyl radiates surety
of vested loss and error. A bus today instead of train, no fault
of the system, naturally. Late, late—the wheels' rough tune
runs on the slow shore detour past gray shacks and split-rail
fences, where old cherry trees bloom thick into salt wind.
I'm wrong again: what's bypassed is not lost, not gone.

One composes in pencil to erase, replace words gone
awry in the moment of patching a semblance of surety.
My son had the courage to write you, an uncle dying, as wind
drops over the Annapolis River. Cowardice is my prime fault;
"too late" my excuse. From bus to train at Shirley, and the rail-
roadbed jolts on to the city. Now engine trouble—that old tune

we hate. I'll be late to work, but deeper guilts tune
out the trivial…. It's two weeks later, and you're gone
in that unknown going, and I again am carried by the sleek rail
as the train moans one long note through the futile surety

of spring's repeated greening. Certainly it's no human fault
that one stands outside another's life bucking its wind—

and won't won't won't admit into one's lungs that wind
of dark: for any, every one some version of the piped-in tune
of glucose, morphine. "O sing ye a new song" in default
of ancient psalm? Not yet possible. I'm going—nearly gone.
Turned over my well-swept house to tenants, without surety
of seed left for the lost bobwhite on his gray deck rail.

Around your garden too a rail fence, and ceaseless wind
lifting into surety of air the birds that twitter a tune
of one life gone, as all, a blameless ending, without fault.

# Contexts

*for H., who gets phone calls,*
*and many like her*

(i)

In rain held off by roof and window,
she, dry, still knows wet,
her mind the lowering gray sky

outside her son's mind. Now she knows
they are statistics, commonplace.
His hard grind has to be greased

by  "stuff" but—
            "not dealing,"
he says, "no needles—"
His phone-voice believes itself,

            so free from referent is the self-
            enclosed world of language.

(ii)

Enough hooey.

He is her son—yes, a sentiment. "He,"
deictic pronoun, floats meaningless. But "son"—
there's context for you.

Dreamt she bore him again, shoved him out
dripping with amnion
full grown, as gray-eyed mind

sprang adult from world-generator's
skull. No myth umbilical hooks
one to one

—so he, sprung from her in utterance's
severance of thought from body.

Not hooked, she knows hooked:
His thought-world skids on tracks
only apparently parallel.

"Son": if only a word could detox—

       (iii)

"Mother" is the overbearing word.

Literature mothers language, molds random
gene-words to the unique production

she grunts out between her legs, then names.
The noun not to be confused with what is named.

It's him, incorrect. Nothing to do with language.
Call these lines "the mother ghazal"

because one never shakes off the form
and role of somebody's mother, but in fact

the same independence exists. He is he.
Fixes travel in his blood that once

was made from hers, so words are circling
uselessly through her:  oh—oh—oh

on a wet night dry labor
that won't deliver him again.

       (iv)

    And heads get hooked on their own forms.
Nightfall means dark wet outside to one
      and to another, warmth of the inner hearth:

It's a party. Her frizz-haired friend
smokes a joint and groans, "I couldn't stand
the guilt. That's why I never had children.

Too afraid. Knew I couldn't bear
the responsibility—"
Indicted, the listener

still believes in the declarative sentence,

brave or deluded says to herself again:
better to have a son than not to have one

.  .  .

But what if he o.d.'s?

(v)

Dark eases in. Eaves drip a little,
a few words drift from the TV—

so thoughts dance across the mind-screen,
breaking down fear and the tired need

to settle fear. Shouldn't she let him fade
from her brain, displaced by imitation swordplay

and British accents in jiggly TV color?
His phone's disconnected now, the night over-quiet.

She sits up till 4 or 5 a.m., as if
her sleeping might let him down, writes him

letters to go possibly unread—
certainly unread, writes in the grip
of the horribly questionable mother-cycle:

yeah, useless—

(vi)

Syzygy these days,
the weatherman announces moon and sun
aligned, and earth

in its ellipse
closest as it can be to the sun—still  93 million
miles away.

Murderous tides
along the coast, moon-pulled, tell us that close
is no better than far.

This storm follows from that near star.

> *This poem is no letter. It has*
> *no end.* Its moebius-strip
> unending surface

slips back into unseen beginning
     in circling water, wet still falling,
          resumption *da capo al fine*

# What Is Coming

(i)

*Piner's Nursing Home, California,*
*Bethesda Care Center, et al.*

What approaches is imageless:
odor of deodorizer at the nursing station,
oxygen cylinder outside a closed door.

A door is closing. A voice
activates a telephone. Temporary
transmission of impulses connects

"mother," "child"—false labels for
the long severed. Memory means severance.
That warning on the bottle

went unread. What approaches
is wordless, the one word too much.
Low slant winter sun shines blank

and blank mind speaks. What must
be known can't be. Do you imagine
pear-blossoms warm in the old orchard,

a cycle counted on as river-circle
underground? Don't. Return's not
endless. What approaches

is new. I dip a cup and bring up
silt to drink. I send words back
to a voice outliving words.

The neural circuitry clicks off.
It will come obliquely, like that. Seem
not to be happening.

After-pulsations image a net
that holds. Spaces between the knots
define the net; thus the void of "mother"

energizes a continent of wires.
Every mother's cord is cut. You forget.
One promises to phone again, not wholly

disbelieving in equipment. Oxygen
is odorless. What approaches isn't.

Isn't. Breathe it in.

(ii)

*4 p.m. in New York*

Snow's clarity which lit up morning windows now
turns faintly gray, reminds—but why do I object?

Lunchtime in California: chicken soup at Piner's.
My mother holds a saltine ladylike in her left hand,

thinks: that old gal over there's completely gone,
but I—why soup for breakfast? Who's this visitor,

my daughter or granddaughter?

My mother introduced me to her roommate.
Then my mother introduced me to her roommate.

Memory is form, holding a self like skin.
It goes, and the person goes, all but a haunted body.

More snowfalls, blue under darkening sky,
simplifying the landscape to gaps and blotches.

I dislike this night's way of looking in at me.
I go round and twist the wands that shut the blinds.

# PART V

# Cloud, Rock, Scroll

# Cloud, Rock, Scroll

*from the Colorado mountains, meditating on H.D., myth-maker,*
*in her sea garden, as dead priestess and as Helen in Egypt*
— "she herself is the writing"

(i)

*Rock Rose*

Wild roses among rocks

in sun-blanched grasses
twine the cabin's split steps.

Petals infold
concealing gold stamens.
Drought crumples them.
Night frost will surely
scatter them—

yet more at morning
bloom among boulders.

Your peony-pink
is stitched on green leaf-brocade
sprung from dust.
How has desert thrust you up?
You are foreigners
born here.

Your silk spins from a harsh worm.
You flare in high wind.
Do your roots reach
down to a hidden river?

*At sundown mountains darken.*
*The sky fills with rose-fire clouds.*

*Rock Lily*

Lily of the rocks,
lily of aspen shadows,
rare mariposa, your ivory petal-cup
streaked with subtlest purple
bends to the meadow
on a single stalk

as a wise woman averts her eyes
not needing praise.

> *Delia of Miletus, priestess,*
> *healer, speaks after death as one*
> *who "stood apart,"*
> *and "sang a secret song."*

Lily of willow springs,
lily of mountain mist,
you are rooted far
from white sand
or temple column—

an offering
without shrine

*(iii)*

*Wraiths*

> *on a trail to tree line*

Fog hides the peaks.
Scarves of mist drift among pines.
The dark boughs drip.

No laurels in these woods,
no spirit's scented flower-breath.
The stream runs cold

and rough.  It speaks
of nothing beyond itself. It eats away
the trail beside it.

Deeper woods.
An old mine-shaft
—human remnant—fills with dirt
under a fallen fir-trunk:

after that no trace
of construct or precursor.
                        Rain begins.

Wet trees stand
in the path, wraiths black but veiled.
I fade into their landscape, insubstantial,

an absence.
No deity, shrine nor scripture,
crucible nor angel
but her seeking mind remembered

and these shape-shifters, pale
behind cracked branches, draw me on—

>    *Rock creates the fall of water,*
>    *air dispersion,*
>    *earth its catch-basin.*
>
>    *Formless runnels*
>    *form cross-trails.*
>    *Mud hollows hold*
>    *a momentary silver*
>    *sky-mirrors,*
>    *light-givers,*
>
>    *incessant*
>    *reformation of water.*

*Sky*

Blue sky of emptiness:
deepest blue    strongest
blue of amethyst, of lapis,

of turquoise buried
under most ancient rock    blue
of transient lupine,

drooping harebell at
lake's rim two miles high in blue
air where fossil shells

imprint the granite—

blue    over these peaks
once sea-bottom, your height

depth endless, "nothing
whatever but everything
comes from it." Water

in blue tarns above
tree line    covers pearly stones
that sink from sight as

mountains rise to hide
in clouds that lie on those blue
mirrors. Sky, water,

rock self-existing,
enmeshed in utter difference,
open mystery:

—"not why it is but
*that* it is," that mind can see

as word and woman

in one hieroglyph:
*she herself is the writing*

—and light to read it.

(v)

*Now*

Light changes:
gray in the cabin window.
Thunder rumbles and the power goes off

a moment. Mountains make weather. Now
hail pummels stovepipe and roof,
then sun, blatant,

creates leaf-shine
in wet scrub oak. This transience,
this rough-walled one plain room, bind

and drive one's thought. Rock roses' bloom
has passed but left leaf and thorn,
grubstake

for another season.

My heroines
work alone. "Mountain Charley"
put on men's clothes, shipped on a Mississippi river-

gambler's boat, went west, panned gold in Victor
and Cripple Creek, sent money
back to St. Louis nuns

for two daughters' convent schooling.
She was eighteen and widowed. She had no way to live

but crudely, in disguise.

                    No myth,
this history hacks itself out in unruly
shapes.

          *My west, how have you written me?*

          .    .    .

          Now you, shape-shifter,
name-changer,
in Helen's white chiton
girdled with purple
of mountain gentian,
               haunt my crude refuge.

          No myth but you,
disguised by names,
initials, images of sea,
wind, sand, of poppy-flame,
you meet my mind
               with mind no place

          but here on uneven
rock that rises
distant to the mountains
shrouded in cloud.

No Fuji or Olympus.
          Still,
*eidolon,* for you
an offering:
                    this effort,
watercolor
of the pale yellow rippled
under-edge of thunderhead,
          sun held a moment in end-glow:

this scroll.

# About the Author

PHOTO: MICHELLE HOOD

Jane Augustine is a poet and scholar with three previous books of poetry, *Night Lights* (2004) and Arbor Vitae (2002), both from Marsh Hawk Press, and *Transitory* from Spuyten Duyvil (2002). Twice a winner of Fellowships in Poetry from the New York State Council on the Arts, she has also published numerous essays on H.D., Lorine Niedecker, and other modern women writers. Her short story, "Secretive," has been anthologized and used repeatedly in women's studies courses. She is the editor of *The Gift by H.D. The Complete Text* (UP Florida, 1998) and has held the H.D. Fellowship in American Literature at Beinecke Library, Yale. Her essay on Mahayana Buddhism and French philosophy appears in *Buddhisms and Deconstructions* (Rowman & Littlefield, 2006). She lives in New York City and Westcliffe, Colorado.

Thomas Fink, *Clarity*

Karin Randolph, *Either She Was*

Norman Finkelstein, *Passing Over*

Sandy McIntosh, *Forty-Nine Guaranteed Ways to Escape Death*

Eileen Tabios, *The Light Sang As It Left Your Eyes*

Claudia Carlson, *The Elephant House*

Steve Fellner, *Blind Date with Cavafy*

Basil King, *77 Beasts: Basil King's Bestiary*

Rochelle Ratner, *Balancing Acts*

Corinne Robins, *Today's Menu*

Mary Mackey, *Breaking the Fever*

Sigman Byrd, *Under the Wanderer's Star*

Edward Foster, *What He Ought To Know*

Sharon Olinka, *The Good City*

Harriet Zinnes, *Whither Nonstopping*

Sandy McIntosh, *The After-Death History of My Mother*

Eileen R. Tabios, *I Take Thee, English, for My Beloved*

Burt Kimmelman, *Somehow*

Stephen Paul Miller, *Skinny Eighth Avenue*

Jacquelyn Pope, *Watermark*

Jane Augustine, *Night Lights*

Thomas Fink, *After Taxes*

Martha King, *Imperfect Fit*

Susan Terris, *Natural Defenses*

Daniel Morris, *Bryce Passage*

Corinne Robins, *One Thousand Years*

Chard deNiord, *Sharp Golden Thorn*

Rochelle Ratner, *House and Home*

Basil King, *Mirage*

Sharon Dolin, *Serious Pink*

Madeline Tiger, *Birds of Sorrow and Joy*

Patricia Carlin, *Original Green*

Stephen Paul Miller, *The Bee Flies in May*

Edward Foster, *Mahrem: Things Men Should Do for Men*

Eileen R. Tabios, *Reproductions of the Empty Flagpole*

Harriet Zinnes, *Drawing on the Wall*

Thomas Fink, *Gossip: A Book of Poems*

Jane Augustine, *Arbor Vitae*

Sandy McIntosh, *Between Earth and Sky*

Burt Kimmelman and Fred Caruso, *The Pond at Cape May Point*

**Marsh Hawk Press** is a juried collective committed to publishing poetry, especially to poetry with an affinity to the visual arts.

Artistic Advisory Board: Toi Derricotte, Denise Duhamel, Marilyn Hacker, Allan Kornblum, Maria Mazzioti Gillan, Alicia Ostriker, Marie Ponsot , David Shapiro, Nathaniel Tarn, Anne Waldman, and John Yau.

For more information, please go to: **http://www.marshhawkpress.org.**